TOKEN
AND
JUJU BEADS

Poetry and Stories of
Reflection & Resilience

TOKEN
AND
JUJU BEADS

Poetry and Stories of
Reflection & Resilience

O'NEIL C PEMBERTON

CITI OF
BOOKS

CITIOFBOOKS, INC.

3736 Eubank NE Suite A1
Albuquerque, NM 871113579
www.citiofbooks.com
Hotline: 1 (877) 3892759
Fax: 1 (505) 9307244

Ordering Information:

Quantity sales. Special discounts are available on quantity purchases by corporations, associations, and others. For details, contact the publisher at the address above.

Printed in the United States of America.

ISBN13:	Softcover	978-1-963209-45-7
	eBook	978-1-963209-47-1
	Hardback	978-1-963209-46-4

Library of Congress Control Number: 2024901455

TABLE OF CONTENTS

i

DEDICATION

I would like to dedicate this book to a few people who have been instrumental in my life.

Hermina Wade, who made me strong and showed me there is more to life than I ever dreamed of.

Richard Shulman, a beloved friend who opened his home and his heart to a poor black kid from the islands.

Phylis Wilkins, a woman who treated me like a son and has always been kind to me.

Jasemen, Fred, Carolina, Dixie, and Henkie welcomed me into their family and will always be part of mine.

Marilyn, my big sister, who shares my early childhood memories.

My wife Maria, who has been the joy of my life, and without her none of these words would have seen the light of day.

Jean and Enrique, who have become my creative partners and have opened my mind to so many possibilities.

To my kids Marcus, Shian, and Aldo, who give me so much joy to see them grow.

To all the people who are by blood or by other means and have become my family.

And finally, to Donna and Carol - I did it!

THANKFUL

There is so much to be thankful for.

The body that God gave me and the health that I have. The air that I breathe.

The people whom I have met, good and bad, have taught me about humanity and the fragility of life.

Family, who are always in my heart wherever they are, blood and otherwise.

The poor, who keep me humble with the ability to learn of my plight and to give more of myself.

My children make me proud even when they are not at their best. For hope in this world that we will one day see peace. My wife shares my good and bad days yet still somehow shows so much love for me.

Most of all I am thankful that I am still here. I wrote most of this book during 2020 and a lot of people did not make it through COVID.

For all this, I am thankful for and more.

INTRODUCTION

As a person of color growing up on the island of Nevis, I read more about the country that I am in now than the one I grew up in. Over time I found that the things that triggered me to want to be in the United States have also made me rethink my earlier choices that were without proper research. Like any immigrant, I wanted the life that I read about and saw on TV. I believed most of it, even the things that were said about my own race and others. It was a learning experience to come face to face with the reality. I realize that what you are told, and what the truth is are two different things. There are good humans in this world, and I have tried to seek them out and engage with them from every background. There is so much beauty (and similarities) in people who you thought that you could never be akin to. I have friends that are from the other side of the globe that when I got to know them, really know them, and their life stories, I realized they are our brothers and sisters, and what they want is the same as any of us - peace, love and family.

My kids will never experience the kind of life I had in Nevis. When I explain to them where I came from and the upbringing I experienced, it's like an alien world to them. Am I sad about it? Yes and No. I want more for them and I want them to see the true value in people. Not for the color of their skin or the background they came from. I want them to be on equal footing and to be graded by their contributions to society. My kids, and hopefully their kids, will keep in mind that we are on this planet and it is getting smaller as it reaches its capacity. The idea is to work in unity to keep this place called earth going for as long as we can, United.

These poems reflect my thoughts and frustrations of the times that we live in and the hurdles we must cross. Some of it is raw and filled with angst, but, it's my true feelings in the moment and to deny what I feel would not be genuine. I intend to be true to myself and my feelings in these works that follow. There is hope and awareness in the work we have ahead of us. I would hope that no one has their head in the sand about the energy and patience we need to heal, and get to a place of liberty and justice for everyone.

As a child I moved around a lot. My mother died when I was 5 and my whole life changed. I was very shy growing up and stuttered a bit. I never felt like I fit in anywhere and I had to learn to navigate life without the guidance of my parents. When I was about 7, I had an accident and ended up with a scar under my eye. I grew up believing that I was ugly, and that the scar defined who I was. People said hurtful things to me that made me doubt my place in the world. Reading remedied all that. I could curl up in a corner and escape the life I was in, and it did not matter what the book was about, I was willing to do anything I could to escape where I was. First, I have to say I love everyone. The is no mal intent for anyone out there, I really, really do care about everyone. People who love one another can disagree and still find common ground. What I am looking for in these pages that follow, is an understanding of my opinion on what is going on around us. I have known what it means to be black all my life and the things that make me aware may be oblivious to some people outside my race. The important thing for me is to share and maybe we can find common ground.

When I went to church as a kid, I was told that "it didn't matter if we were red or yellow or black or white -- we are special in his sight." All this seems to have changed as adults in America. I believe that God would not accept what is going on right now in the world. The police brutality, wars over land, hate of immigrants, no tolerance for others political points of view . . . we are all struggling with what to feel, but turning away and not having empathy is not being a good Christian (or human).

I want to share that that police brutality has hurt me to the core. I have seen it and I have experienced it. It evokes a time from the past when we were killed and brutalized with impunity. In this time and age, we could do better. Anyone who goes out, looting and causing violent acts should stop, yet I understand their frustration. If you are backed up in a corner, the only option sometimes is to fight. Don't let this divide us because we are one people and what people of color want is the same as anyone else. Open your eyes to what is happening outside of your safe zone, and you will be alarmed and disgusted. Because if you and your kids were in that situation you would do what is right and speak up against it. I want a better life for my kids and that's why I have to speak up.

LEAVING HOME

I knew it would come yet when it happened it was almost like an out of body experience, a dream. Something that would wake me up and I would cry about because it was not real, but I was now leaving home.

There were no set plans or calculated ideas, it was just something that I knew I had to do, and the means of doing it was the least of my worries. There was nothing left in Nevis for me. The beauty that the foreign tourists came to see year after year was not something I had an appreciation for anymore. All the memories piled in my head, and held on to, most so bad that they were painful to recreate, but I held on to them because this is what would build my determination to never return. All the people I met, the painful existence that I endured, the friends that I went to school with will be replaced, not the memories but the people. New memories, with better outcomes is what I hoped for.

After high school there was no direction. My friends who could afford it were off to someplace better to finish their education, to prepare for a better life. I just grasped at anything that was thrown at me and survived by my wits and optimism, hoping and waiting for something or someone to reach out and give me a new lease on life, a lifeline.

The options for work in Nevis were terrible -- construction, fishing, farming, storekeeper, or drugs. None of these seemed like a pathway to anywhere good or worthwhile, and I had witnessed boys who were brilliant in high school reduced to drinking and waiting for some relative back in the states to send back a barrel of goods, or something, from wherever they went to.

I had other plans because I could not do any of these. I had to get off this beautiful hellhole and make a life that I could be happy with in old age. Not to squander the last of my brain cells as an old man in some bar trying to erase the feelings of a dream I had. No, not me, I am going, and I am going soon before the monotony of this life and the pull of failure holds me there.

I could have joined the navy but the idea of giving my life to get a life did not appeal to me. I wanted it to be on my own terms and the life I had was already given to others since the age of 5. I have to see what my limits were, and I have to leave to do that.

I had no ties to anything. I did not own anything, and no one had a claim to me, so I was free to do whatever I pleased at an age when boys had to be accountable to their parents and family. I did not have either. I was free but so lost. The smile and happy laughter hid so much pain that I felt, like I was drowning on dry land most of the time.

The opportunity came unexpectedly, and I scrambled to get the paperwork I needed to leave. There were questions in my mind whether the intent of my savior was innocent and heartfelt. There was not a whole lot to pack. The photo that was on my passport I was wearing one of the few shirts that I owned, and that one in particular was the one that I wore daily to school. I would come home and take it off and wash it and hang it on the line to dry for the next day. My body was changing and I was getting bigger, but that shirt lasted until the last day of school. I went home that day and brought my elbow together and the back of the shirt tore in two like paper. The armpits were stained from so many days of me wearing it in the hot tropical weather. My pants, a pair of brown Gaberdine, had on many occasions split at the crotch and I had gone home, got needle and thread out, and got them ready for the next day. My savior was that it was a uniform, so I blended in even with the ill fitted form. Shoes were another thing that was a luxury and I held on to mine by any means necessary, sliding cardboard inside to walk in them. There were days I could not wait to get home so I could take them off because they were 2 sizes too small. I never felt embarrassed or ashamed. I covered all those feelings and inadequacies with humor, and I would be the first to make fun of me. I never gave anyone else the chance to. Plus, I did not care, I knew someday I would leave.

First time on a plane, and the first time I was going anywhere of significance. The most traveling I had done up to that point was the ferry that I had taken on occasion to visit my sister who lived on the neighboring island of St. Kitts, or taking the bus from the town to the country maybe 12 miles away. My sister was older, and her father had taken her in when our mother died. My life was a lot different from hers. I went to live with my father who was married, and I was the young bastard child his wife would see and scorn every day. I tried my best to stay away and maintain a distance, but I was reminded that my father had strayed and the punishment was to be parceled out to me in small, unexpected increments. There was no hiding any of the anger she had towards me and I took it as long as a young innocent boy could. Not knowing my options until it became too much, and in a daring move, I left the house at age 13 because I could not take the treatment anymore.

Maybe I was stubborn or just foolish, but I depended on the kindness of strangers and friends. I worked odd jobs and still went to school although I was homeless. There were many nights that I was so hungry that I would steal some food just to get my stomach to stop grumbling. I remember being able to pull my belly in and it would almost hit my backbone. Through all this I held on to the hope that if I just stayed focused, I could get through this.

Books and laughter were my escape, but sometimes the laughter was not real. I had to pretend that my life, this life I lead was something to laugh at. I remember going to a graduation party, but not like the other kids my age. I was the one outside peeking through the shutters as the other kids inside had a great time. I never told anyone the real reason I could not go, but instead made excuses. I held it all in and did not share the dismay and fear I had to someday be that guy who would stumble home drunk from disappointment.

The transition to America was hard. The life I had in Nevis and the life I was now living was on a different spectrum. Where I came from, a place that was hot, with beaches and a laid-back lifestyle in comparison to the place I was in, it was cold, damp and fast paced. I came to America during November and didn't understand why all the plants were dead and why it was cold all the time. Lack of planning and not having a realistic view of what to expect threw me for a loop. Months on end I thought I would be better off back home. It was cold all the time and nothing that I wore seemed to make me warm enough. I missed the island life, plus the independence I had. I now had to be accountable to someone all the time. Things were off balance and the dreams I had were slowly being demolished.

It took the support of a friend in America to get me back to where I felt some hope. Living in a place where at any time, I could be sent back was always on my mind. Just talking to someone with the knowledge to navigate the system was foreign to me.

It took me a while, but the new life started to grow on me. I felt that I was becoming. Becoming what; I did not know, but it was a chance for me to reinvent myself. I chose a new name, the change was good, and I lived with the decision to leave the past behind and all the changes that came with it.

That changed on a Sunday morning, I saw a face from the past on Facebook, and thought I would reach out. I tried to get a friend request but after a few days of no reply I sent him an old picture of himself from years ago. We had been close and, on many occasions, had spent time at the beach and on the street corner hanging out. We had reconnected on a brief visit I had some decades back. He was still there trying to get a footing into the world of culinary arts and working at the hotels. We had talked about the new hotel that was being built and I could see his excitement in getting a job there.

After a few days and no reply, even after the picture of him from years back. I wrote, it's me, remember me, I lived close to you, and you knew my brothers. Nothing, then a one-line reply, send more pictures. That was it.

It took me a while to realize that 30 plus years has gone by and here I am, a ghost from the past reaching back to retrieve something that will never return to me. Young men with dreams and willing to cut ties, but in old age reminiscent on friendship that has gone stale, and the span between is so wide that we had nothing relatable to talk about.

I had given up all that. I am not that kid anymore and my struggles are of another kind. I eat well, have a place to sleep and have built a life that I wanted. But here I am with all that I have, reaching back for old friends who I have held at arm's length. I never wrote letters or kept in touch. My pain was too much to bear and going back even in idle talk would make it too painful, so I cut everything and everyone out. But it all came at a cost as I sit here thinking of my friends from when we were all hungry for more.

LETTERS FROM HOME

It took me a few days to open the letter that had been placed on my side table. I knew it would be an emotional roller coaster hearing about words from home. My life has not been easy in America and the feeling of homesickness was always close to the surface. It's been 10 years since I left Nevis, and it did not take much for my mind drift to the beach, woods and alleyways that I roamed as a kid.

The letters from Grannie always started with the same salutation and greetings.

"Hi son how have you been? For me I ..." and it would go on to explain all the ailments that she suffered from. There was an endless amount of guilt that I felt because I was not there to comfort and take care of the woman that replaced the mother that I knew only for a few years.

Growing up she was everything to us, my sister and me. She was the boss lady who almost never emitted a smile and showed no remorse in her punishments and acts of discipline. Now seeing her frail and complaining about her maladies made her a different person. Now the smiles were often and the last time I did get to see her there were even more hugs.

The letter went on to talk of everything that was related to her and the people around even though it's been 10 years as if I just left yesterday.

"They are fixing the road going to Jessup" and "I saw one of your school mates and he said to tell you hi."

Maybe it was embarrassment or not wanting to be compared to someone elses path that they choose, but I had cut all ties to the friends I left behind. I did not want to explain the circumstances of my life living here in the States. They would not understand or at least I think they would not. I was in America; that would mean to anyone of my old friends there on the island that I was rich. America -- that was the place to be. It was almost like heaven to them. You have all those nice clothes and fancy restaurants. What was there to complain about? I took the letter in my hand, it was in a small white envelope with a red, blue and black lined border. The Queen looks back at me from the stamp, and although a small envelope it was crammed tight. Oh boy I said to myself. She must have a lot to say this time.

My grandmother lived in England for years and yet she held on to all the traditional things she knew a woman growing up on the island. I remember on one of her visits and making sure that she had enough space in her suitcase to put her "bush tea." There was one for this and one for that and I thought how ridiculous it is to come from a country with all its wealth to take back some bush tea? These were the things that now that I am here in America, I tried to eliminate from my life. I later learned that most of the tea she took back had more medical power than most of the pharmaceutical drugs from a doctor. I remember her visits to Nevis when I was younger and she would seek out the local bush doctor so she could procure the best treatment for her arthritic pain. Mind you she was coming from Great Britain, a place I would guarantee would have better medicine and health care than a back woods bush doctor. But here she was stuffing her suitcase of local medicine. Her heart and soul never left home, and I was determined not to follow in her footsteps.

The first few years I was in the States I wrote a few letters to friends and family and gradually all the connections were slowly severed. Many times, I told myself, I have to in order to integrate into my American life. This was my new home and I had to fit it. There was no way in hell I was going back. I had to succeed in doing this. There was limited options back there for me.

As I tore the envelope open, I took care not to do too much damage since I knew I would keep it with the others stacks of letters that she had written me before.

It was my way of having her close. Throwing away the read letters would be like discarding a treasure that could not be replaced. Years later I would scan those letters and hear her voice in my head. "Son, have respect and be nice to the family you are staying with. Be a good boy please." My situation was a little unique since I did not have any family in this country and my living situation was taken on by the goodness of strangers. This makes life sometimes a little bit tricky. There was no fallback to a relative's home or apartment.

If I was not on my best behavior, I could be homeless or even worse sent home.

As I read some of what she wrote she was describing how my aunt was doing, and how she was not getting around as much anymore. And, "but thank God I am still here, praise the lord, to see you doing fine. We are going to be just fine."

As she wraps up her letters, she wanted to let me know who died. "Remember Griffin up the street next to Thompson. Well, they did not see him for a few days, and someone went to his house and he had died. They had to call his kids in St. Thomas the big island and let them know. Blackie Funeral Home came and took him, I notice his son Wilfred was with him. I think he went to school with you, and they had a nice service for him. They buried him over by the Anglican Church in Gingerland not far from where your mother is buried."

I knew the spot. As a child I had to go to this church which I had to walk for miles to get there. I would walk by the small churches closer and wonder why we have to go to this church so far away. We never questioned it out loud because it was not something you would even mention as a kid. You are going to this church and that was that. The ordeal of going to church until this day leaves me dreading ever going again. But I would never say that to my grandmother who thought that the more church you go to the better you become. Sundays were truly a day about the Lord growing up.

It would start Saturday evening when she would start cooking and all your clothes were taken out and pressed for church. Going to church was no joke and unless you were laid up in the hospital you are going to church. During the week I would run around bare foot but on Sunday you had to squeeze your feet into that patent leather shoe, and if it hurts, you bear it until you get home. That long walk with a button up shirt and sometimes a jacket with my clip-on tie. This was a nightmare for me. My hair had to be combed and I hated combing my hair so my sister would do it, and it was as if your head was on fire when she was done with you. All the knots and snags that I accumulated during the week were dragged from my head whether I liked it or not. Grannie's kids would not go to church looking like a ragamuffins. By the time we got there we were already tired and hot and dying for the whole thing to be over. But when we got back home we had a short break and then off to Sunday school.

The letter went on about people who went to the hospital and people who have not been seen for a while. All ending with her telling me to "take care of yourself and say hi to everyone and God bless."

It was a piece of home here in a cold, sometimes wet and overcast place, that felt like a million miles from the sun and beach that I grew up on. I have to let it go or at least put it away or I will go insane.

I missed a lot of things that I left behind, but those small reminders make it even worse, and I couldn't go back then. My life was just getting started here.

I folded the letter just as how she had sent it and turned it around in my hands a few times thinking what the hell am I doing here? Tears welled up in my eyes and I wiped them away and straightened up my back. Next month I will be moving into my own place and

I have to pass on to her my new address so that she could send me more letters of news from home.

SLOW DECLINE

It's Sunday morning, and the young orphan boy will be coming soon. He was coming to help with all the chores that Miss Saline could not, or would not, do anymore. She was a beauty once, she told herself, as she caught a glance of herself in the mirror as she made her way to the window. He will be here soon, and I want to make sure he knows I am here. As she looks back at herself and her thinning hair, she would not be caught dead without one of her multiple wigs that she had neatly stowed away in boxes in her closet. Getting old is such a drag. All the people that you knew either are dead or will not return your call. Plus, having lost her husband, who ultimately was the means and access to the lifestyle she now held on to desperately.

There was a time when she was the talk of the town. A trophy wife to a man who had wealth and status. Well, she was a second wife to a man who could afford to keep her in decent clothes, but she had an illusion to maintain, and she intend to keep it up as long as she could.

Since he died all the children from his first marriage just seemed to be hovering, waiting for her to die, knowing that the property and all the contents would be theirs. He never told her anything about the money he had. She was so happy to have met a man who could shower her with stuff and the status that she had gained. The high tea at the club, meeting people who were in high regard like government officials who ran the country. They were always respectful but now he is gone they smile and offer condolences but the invitation to events soon dried up and people now don't return her call. The ladies, wives of executives and ministers of government affairs who she mingled with in the old days seemed to have gone underground.

She had tried desperately to hold on to that look of opulence and wealth, but she was nearly broke and she had quietly been selling things to buy food and maintain the property that she lived in.

There is a lot you could do with yourself that give people the air that you are wealthy, but the house was hard to maintain with the money she had left. It was either food or paint, and she was not about to go hungry, plus the house was not even hers. It was to be passed on to his kids who seem to make her always aware that she was a guest and death was the next exit.

The grass that was once maintained, almost to the look of carpet, stayed green even on the hottest tropical days when the temperature would be 80 plus for weeks on end. They called it sponge grass because it bounced when you walked on it like a sponge carpet. There were beautiful flower trees in the yard and a large mango tree that shaded a part of the wrap around veranda.

On the veranda at night, she would sit in the darkness and listen to the idle gossip of people who walked by who were unaware she was there in the dark. There was no light on in the house at night unless she was going from one room to another, and it gave people the impression that the house was empty. Many times the neighborhood boys would jump the fence to steal the mangoes that fell under the tree, sometimes she would make a noise to see them scatter like rats out of the yard. Other times, just because she knew she could not clean the mess of the fallen ripe mangoes, so she would just watch saying nothing. They were unaware that she knew they were there. A few times she had let the cat out of the bag when on her trip to the market she would see someone who had stolen her mangoes selling them at their stall. She never made a fuss of it but made sure they were aware she knew where the mangoes came from. She knew if she had made it an issue, she would have to hire someone to clean up under the tree because there were so many mangoes.

The outside steps going to the second floor were in such disrepair you have to stay close to the wall of the house and walk very gingerly on the creaking boards.

One of these days the whole side is going to fall but she was not going to put a dime into any repairs. She was going to be 68 this year and lord knows how many more years the little money she has will last. Those greedy kids of his will not benefit from any of the money he left behind for me, she said to herself.

There was always the thought of marriage again. To find someone who maybe was in need of a companion. It gets lonely sometimes but the idea of putting herself out there in a public way was way too daunting for her. She went through so much with her late husband. His family always looked at her as a money grabbing bitch and maybe she was, but she was the one who gave up her beauty to lay next to a man who was almost twice her age. She has a feeling of regret but when life was good it was very good. All of her friends who she grew up with thought she was a success because she was hobnobbing with people who held lots of power and she was not afraid to name drop or mention some of the places she was able to visit, or dignitaries who she had come in contact with. She would flaunt her good fortune whenever the opportunity arose without any shame.

Those years were good until his health started to decline, she had to spoon feed him in bed and as he came to the end, change his soiled underwear. She could have left, but by then the beauty that she once was were showing signs of cracks. And who would have her knowing she left a man when he was in the September of his life. So, she held on hoping he would die soon enough while she had something yet to trade.

Ten years of doing that and you watch your life just drift away and bitterness set in. When it got too much, the smell of a man slowly dying in a room that you have not shared a bed with in over 10 years, gets to you. There were tears and she had thoughts of getting a lover. The little confidence that she had slowly weaned as the years went by.

Socially it was a nightmare since if you were seen out, people would gossip about you not taking care of your man. "How can she do that while her husband lay dying at home," she could hear them saying. It became more of a burden to go anywhere with the guilt of having left the house with her bed-ridden husband at home.

On a small island community, it's hard to go about your business without being judged.

Well, we all made our beds and I guess this is mine, she said to herself as she busied herself to get all that mess of life out of her head. "It will be just fine" she said to herself. I still have some jewelry that is worth something and if I can hold on, I will make it through this without resorting to begging she thought.

I also have some nice Persian rugs and beautiful furniture that I could sell for some cash if need be. Most of the people around here have never seen stuff like this. It was not made by some shoemaker who thought he could make furniture. These were handmade in America by skilled carpenters out of the finest Mahogany with a high shine poly finish. "Solid pieces that I picked out myself and I know a thing or two about decorating" she thought. That was one of the things that he allowed me to do. All I had to do was smile and wink and he would write a check. I was a trophy that you want to keep on a mantle, happy and content. It tells your friends that you are a man of means to have a beautiful young wife. All you had to do was satisfy her spending habits, but at the same time, keep it in check. She was given an allowance, plus if she wanted anything else she just has to ask. He was generous and now she realized that she should have been more aware that she could be in a situation like this. She should have had a secret account and been more resourceful so she could exit whenever she wanted. But that never came to mind because she thought the good life would last forever and she would be generously compensated for all the years she put it. Now she has to admit she was wrong. Here she is squeezing every penny to keep face so that she is not ridiculed by the people around her. It's always show time for her. She had to maintain a sense of pride in order to keep one thing intact, her dignity.

"Where is that boy? He should have been here by now," she grumbled to herself. Why worry about the past? This is the life I have now, and I have to accept it. So much for my life before, I am still here, and I will make the best of it. It will soon be time for me to leave this earth anyways. I will die knowing that I have maintained my dignity and what little self-respect I have worked so hard to maintain. It will be over soon.

Your Inheritance

There is blood on the path you walk on.
The blood of my forefathers who came before me,
when the great spirits were close
and they could hear me.
Now here you are walking on my inheritance.
I do not fear you,
but what you have done to my great nation,
my people,
we are the curators of Mother Earth.

Sit Still And Listen

As a child I was told to sit still and listen.
But the curiosity of a child was in me, and my mind wandered.
There was too much around me to be discovered.
So, I was told again and again, sit still and listen.
All the world was new to me,
there was the chatter of voices here and there
telling me to sit still and listen.
It never occurred to me that my inner self was saying the same thing.
So many questions, until adulthood when the noise became a clatter of losses and gains,
which forced me to sit still and listen.
When aged and in our quiet September, all we have is time to sit still and listen to the beauty that surrounds us.
The beauty, so much beauty, that was missed
if only we had sat still and listened.

HANGING HERE

I'm hangin here and I ain't got to pick any cotton no mo

They decided I ain't good for nothin

So, they left me here a hangin

But I ain't got to pick any cotton no mo.

My hand don bled it last bit a blood on Mr. Johnson's field

So, I here and glad cause I ain't got to pick any cotton no mo

Me Pickney gonna miss me but they gonna be ok to know I ain't gonna suffer no mo.

Cause I ain't got to pick any cotton no mo

Don't need no mo vittles and I ain't even hungry no mo since I been hanging here thinking

I ain't got to pick any mo cotton no mo

Da got me a sleeping fo I was too tired a picking dem cotton but now I ain't got to pick any cotton no mo

Too tired a movin and never gettin any further than that their field that's why I a hangin here but I ain't got to pick any cotton no mo

Da thought I a crazy when I smile in da faces when they drag me to this here places but I ain't got to pick any mo cotton no mo

Da hit me with switches but I keep on a smilin cause I ain't got to pick any cotton no mo

My body a need a resting so das why I hanging here thinking I ain't ever want to pick no cotton no mo.

Nice White People

So nice

So, so nice

You are not like the others

You know the ones

The ones who grab their purse

The ones who step off the curb

The ones who say bad things

No, you are not like the others

You want to invite us in, but don't come too often

Don't come at night because what would the neighbors think?

So, nice

We go to the same church but never come to my house

There is always an excuse

So, nice

I could send my kids over but your kids can't come by my house

You get to send your kids to that nice school

but when I moved in your neighborhood you disapproved

But ever so nicely
You explain the reason why
in a way that's not uncomfortable for me
So nicely, that I nod
Agreeing, but yet understanding
Us nice white people you say, want to help but ....
Again…. you put it so nicely
Graduation comes and my son asks your
daughter to the prom and so nicely you decline
So sweet, so nice
But I understand
I understand the comfort you have but will not share
Always helpful, at an arm's length
Always willing to put a band aid on a gushing wound
I watch you and see how you have wrapped things up ever so nicely
Such good white people.

Don't Save Me

Don't wield your hypocrisy for your ill-gotten deeds,

save them for times when logic and foresight is in play.

This realm you call your own could be beaten

down to sand like the castle that it sits on.

There is no fear here,

I will not quiver in the night or be an idle passerby who side steps

your advances.

You will feel my presence although your earthly wealth is greater

than mine.

I will equalize you with will, and show no mercy or resolve.

The blood that runs in my veins are generations strong.

All the inequalities that my forefathers held close to their vest will

be a volcano in my hands.

There will be no retreat.

There will be no surrender.

Until we lay spent and equal in our thinking.

Who You Are?

You are who you are because nothing was given.

There was no silver spoon or comfort from adults

that allowed me to grow but still be nested.

You are who you are because the word "no" was a match, that lit

an amber, that turned into a flame.

What kind of man would you have been if at every turn

there was a hand to guide you?

You are who you are because the pain made you strong and

able to realize that it too will pass.

You are who you are because your willingness to endure and never

yield to all who stood in your way.

Be thankful that all you have accomplished was because the others

were too weak to withstand the journey.

That's who you are.

MOTHER OF MINE

Mother of mine,
whose breast has fed
and hand with goodness led me.
Never weary of kindness so giving to a child.
The roots of the earth and giver of life.
Mother of mine,
so laden with love where words are not enough to express.
Like oceans in millions,
the love for that mother of mine.

TETHERED HERE

Tethered here, between this life and the unknown.

The last goodbyes so often and close.

I lay down my weary shell of a body,

now weak and I am at peace with all I have become.

Legs that held me with grace and wonder

now buckle with the stain of my frail body.

Eyes once bright, take will to see now beyond my hands,

a misty blur.

My blood that once sustained me now leaves me weak and feeble.

What have I become?

My youthful spirit is trapped within me and I long to be free.

That tether that holds me here,

wills me to cut the cord,

freeing me to wander.

MOTHER'S BOY

Years have passed
yet I am my mother's little boy.
Her hands warm and loving
brought me into this world.

There Will Be A Time

There will be a time

when we will face God and repent for a life lived.

Let us in that time of fear and suffering

know and remember we were loved and the spirit we shared.

Will never dies.

We are one again.

MY DREAMS

My dreams are not lofty and filled with self-grandeur.
They are simple with quiet contemplation of happiness.
The sounds and smells that fill me with joy;
Hearing children playing;
Family gathered to celebrate relationships that a house is built on.
Those quiet peaceful moments,
when life stands still for me alone and the world is well.
My dreams are simple . . .
health, love and happiness.

No Bloodline

We are not blood,

but the vein that connects us is strong.

Whatever days and lifetimes lay ahead of us,

our names will be forever linked as a bond.

Yet name alone will not be the solitary link.

We will be bonded by our love and endurance of each other.

The simple deeds to show we love,

and want to be loved.

Let this be our connection to our bloodline.

HERMINA

This life so fleeting and short,
but the love you have given blooms like flowers.
You, Hermina, have lived a good life
and there are flowers that are blooming all around you.
The people you met, the love you have given and the
 memories you have shared.
If there is eternal life, then you have earned it.
As you have aged, your continued compassion and warmth to
those around you have made us feel like being home.
When you are released from this earth
to your heavenly paradise, go knowing
that you have left a field of flowers to bloom.
The sun will rise tomorrow and you will be at home with
your Lord in the kingdom he has prepared for you.
All the beauty of this earth
and its worldly sorrows for you will be no more.
Watch over us with your loving spirit and rest now.

PASSING THROUGH

We have to let go some day.

In this life, we love and hold on to the ones we love.

My hope is that there is a place where we will have a reunion

and say our proper goodbyes.

It's never easy, but one day

we all have to go our separate ways.

I wish I could give up something for your pain

to see you smile at me once again.

But in this life, we can't reach back into the past.

And the moments of laughter go by so fast.

Such cruel consequences of fate

that we come to happiness so late. . . so fleeting.

Fruit Of My Labor

Sit with me my friend

Enjoy tea with me and look at the meal prepared

The fruit of my labor

This land that bears fruit and grain

Lush in harvest

What joy it is to enjoy with friends,

the fruit of our labor

SLY DOG

You sly dog,
You won't make me say something I regret.
There is another route.
I will smile and let your words hang there.
Meaning known, but disguised as a jest.
Smile, that inner voice says . . . just smile.
This won't be the last time,
you will hear the words again.
But don't show your cards yet . . . just smile.
Fix your eyes on what's in front of you.
They know what you could not say.
And yet the game is on.
You will sleep with the sheep tonight and reap your reward
another time.
You sly dog . . . just smile.

Loss Of Morality

We wield our morality like swords,
sharp with disdain for all that sees us.
In youth we are taught to love thy neighbors as ourselves,
but as adults we see the injustices with a blind eye
as we migrate to corners that were created.
The things we preach become hypocrisy.
Our morals only come out when our corners are breached,
and we cling to what was given,
and what was taken with false gestures.
We are human and flawed in every way, yet we contradict
ourselves and find roots on sandy grounds.
Build forts to protect what is not ours,
steal what is not given,
desecrate what we cannot have.
Squander our precious time here.
And that morality that was so preciouses as a child,
and the good book that we read,
now is used to plunder what was never ours.
We are human, and yet we have morals that fit like a suit

and change like the weather.

Watered down to please ourselves,

blinded by the glitter of riches.

The saints now live their lives in castles built for kings.

What a sad refrain we reap.

THE LOVE YOU GIVE

The years are like rings of sediment carved into rocks.
They are the times that show the beginning,
and the future that lays ahead.
Even in disruptive times, we stay stable
and add to the natural progression of our lives.
Time has passed and memories are shared,
and we hold to what remains,
Our love.
Here now in the chapter of our life yet unwritten the future is
bright because of
Our love.
And as we settle in on golden pond,
reflective of what was accomplished,
the gains,
the losses.
We will remember
Our love
and the love that you give to me.

KIKI SAID SO

The woman who bore him into this world
is royalty in my eyes.
Who would say otherwise, even in the presence of his mother?
That smile knew tears but laughter has become
her constant companion now.
I know this because Kiki said so.
I see it in his eyes when he speaks of her,
with a sparkle that I imagine just like hers.
The pride that polishes his words as he lights up
as if ordained to speak of her.
I know this because Kiki said so, many times.
Her travels,
Her upbringing,
Everything about her,
She is royalty surely in the way he speaks of her.
The love shared from a son to a mother and royalty reign.
I know this because Kiki said so.

Hey Aubrey, What Are You Running From?

Is it the knee that rested on your brother Floyd,
until he called for his mother in that final moment?
Hey Aubrey, what are you running from?
Must be the sudden shot, which was not a taser
that got your brother Daunte Wright.
Another son who won't go home tonight
Hey Aubrey, what are you running from?
Must be those skittles packed tight
and you know it's not right to be walking through a
neighborhood that's white at night.
That's why my brother Treyvon Martin is not here anymore.
Hey Aubrey, what are you running from?
All those gone too soon and too many to mention.
Black men and women who died with good intention.
Hey Aubrey, what are you running from?
Is it the ghost of Emmitt Till?
Or our brother Shaheed Vassell?
There are too many of our people gone.
This whole thing has been happening before we were born.

Maybe that is why you are still running.

Hey Aubrey,

I think I know what you are running from.

LETTER TO EMPLOYER

Motherfucker I quit!!

I quit not because the hours do not suit me or the work is too much. I quit because I came to a job that I have to work twice as hard to be recognized.

I quit because when you hired me it was not because of my skill set, my mannerisms, or anything to do with my overall knowledge. I was hired because I am a quota, and that's why I quit.

The years I put in with you group of motherfuckers, who think it's funny to victimize the people they serve, mostly black and brown people.

I sit in your presence, silent because I needed this job.

I have kids and family to support so I hold my tongue and smile as I blow up inside.

I quit this fucking job because if I was treated like any other white worker, I wouldn't have these problems.

But I have to be more, and I am tired of that shit, so I quit.

You there, high and mighty in your clean, well-kept office with the expectation for me to come and clean up your motherfucking mess at the beginning and end of the day.

You're one of the reasons I fucking quit.

I quit because if you really wanted to do your job, you would look around and see that you are no help.

You have perpetuated the myths about black people and people of color.

"Shiftless niggers don't want to work for shit. All they want to do is collect food stamps and smoke weed."

You motherfucker!

I know that's what you think of me.

Good niggers like me take it and say,

"yes Massa, could I have another?"

"Sure thing Massa, you sure are right."

You don't need me to validate your implicit bigotry.

You racist motherfucker!

That's why, motherfucker I quit.

I can't stand another day being your house nigger and agreeing with you while you berate my people.

I can't fucking take it anymore and that's why I fucking quit.

Take your no-good fucking ass and clean your own shit, plow your own land, pick your own fucking fruits.

Take all the shit jobs that you are not willing to pay me for,

so I have to take not one, but maybe two or three jobs,

just to make ends meet.

That's why motherfucker, I quit.

Get off your lazy, high tone ass and take care of your own goddamn kids!

Mow your own fucking lawn!

Cook for your own goddamn kids, because motherfucker I quit.

You are going to get your hands dirty, so get used to it
but I don't give a flying shit because I quit.
Fuck you! and fuck all you stand for.
Now get the fuck out of my way because I FUCKING QUIT!!

Author's Note: You know those days that you wish you could approach your employer and give him a piece of your mind and then quit, well this was one of those days. I felt unappreciated and helpless. This is what came out of me at that moment. I did not quit.

Before Or After?

When do you grieve?

Do you grieve the loss that is to come?

Or hold tight to the moment that you have been given?

Do you wrench your soul, when although diminished, the body remains?

Do you wear black to a visit and remind the living that death lingers at their door?

Or do you brighten their days with bright colors and promise of laughter?

The tears you shed, is it for the burden of loss,

Or the joy and warmth of knowing you soon will go?

Will the flowers you bring smell of death or a chance of another spring?

Will the food taste sour or be filled with the freshness of the moment that may never be repeated?

When the sun goes down, will the shades be drawn and tears flow? Or will the memories in dreams bring a smile and a new tomorrow? Will the years be wasted in suffering, unnecessarily since you are still here?

Or will it be carved with hope and joy of expectation to meet again someday?

My Tears Are Not For You

You mistook my tears for loss, but maybe it isn't.
Maybe instead it is the loss of you
telling me how to think.
Maybe it's the gradual feeling
that I am coming into my own and
what you told me before has lost its meaning.
Maybe instead it's the loss of feeling
as my soul ignites again and
the passion comes back like a lost friend.
Maybe instead it's the fear,
where once I could pass blame for not being in
control of destiny, now I am.
These tears are not shed for simple things,
but maybe it's me finding my voice
and discovering me.
That person that I once was is what I weep for, not you.
With joy.
I am whole again.

I Wanted

I wanted to say something to her
Something vile and insidious
Something that she would understand
Something like what she made me live through
My kindness has been worn thin and
I can only think of hurtful ways to respond
Was it my fault?
Was it something I did?
Were there signs of weakness on my part?
Signs that gave permission to drag me through
a gauntlet of painful interactions?
I should have known.
I should have turned the other way.
Maybe I would not be here, seething with displeasure,
wondering if the words that I want to say will hurt.
Caring about this human being,
with a mother's love she isn't capable of.
Although I can only imagine her in my situation,

exploiting every gasp of air I breathe,

I will remember this moment.

She will hurt me like so many times before.

Then I looked at my son,

and he to me,

and I hold it in.

The hurt I want to give will only hurt him.

It will have to wait.

MOON

This moon will rise for me once more,
and with the rise of the sun
I will be home.
Gone from this earth to sit with my father
in the kingdom he had prepared for me.
All the beauty of this earth
and the worldly sorrows will be no more.
I will watch over you perched in my spirit world,
watching and waiting for you.

In Youth

Reliving our youth and returning to the years when boys,
not yet men, struggle with our destiny.
It seems so far away now.
We would gather and dream together,
and show not a care for a future so bleak and parent like.
It seems so far away now.
The days would go on forever and we would squander them.
Everything seems so far away.
And the fullness of our youthful lives keeps us
wandering like fools.
It seems so far away now.
The constant and relentless needs of adults reflect in us,
the need to mend what they have ruined in their live's years past.
It seems so far away now.
Long hair and tempers short, dirty clothes and dirty minds.
We were invincible then.
It seems so far away now.
Now here, reflecting on my youth,
I am reminded of the time I have,
and it does not seem so far away now.

DID YOU?

Did you earn the scars that manifest themselves in your psyche?
Or did you tether yourself to an ideology that suits you?
Did you do the work to not look back at mistakes made,
or are you a sheep to follow the wolf into its den?
What of your children, like osmosis,
digest your foolish endeavors?
Again, did you do the work of men
who died to protect a freedom, garnished by greed,
and with insufficient time to harvest?
Did you do the work so that we, as individuals, and country
survive what is promised for so many?
The interpretation of words from a charlatan
that stands in your midst.
Soft hands,
fresh smell of false success,
demeaning to those who do not listen to him
and question his validity.
Did he do the work and is he willing
to sacrifice his time to learn the trade?
I am just asking for a friend.

HOME

There will be a time when we all chose
to settle in for the long winters.
Here in my confine,
I will reflect on a joyous youth.
Here I will lay my burden down at night
in this space that I call home.
Where family in future time will gather
and pay homage to days gone by.
All the remnants that surround me will have a story,
which in good company I will share
with a wisp of a smile,
a memory will flutter from years gone by,
and in my heart it will evoke
the feeling that this is my home.
This is where I will make peace with the night
and dream of what's to come.

THESE DAYS

There are days when the words come like raindrops,
torrential and unformed.
And with a tight grasp I sort my feelings,
hoping that the net I cast will be wide enough
to paint the picture I see.
Those days are many,
when in general labor it comes in a flourish
and then disappears.
Seldom I am drawn to anger
because the beauty that is so fleeting etches a mark
upon my soul and I am thankful.

REVERENCE

There is no room here for you to be held in reverence
You are common on this soil until proven otherwise
Treat this day as your first and also your last
You cannot hide behind bloodline or name dropping
There is no need
Heuristic advances will be your only means of transaction
You are common on this soil
Until you have proven yourself worthy of words
from strangers and neighbors alike
Until they hail you with goodwill and
laude your name in remembrance
Until then, you are common on this soil
Mired to sleep
To eat
To toil
In the monotonous life you create, like other souls
who are likeminded and wishful in their pursuit
The strength and perseverance you show over time
will make you more,
but for now
you are common on this soil.

I Am Getting Old

It never occurred to me
But as the days go by in passing conversation,
I notice I am getting old
Reference is made to things that cannot be related to
by someone younger, and I wonder
Is it me or is it something else?
And then I realize
I am getting old
I see the places that I used to go and the changes in the
demographics, and I remember the place as a shopping mall,
a skating rink, a video store and then I realize
I am getting old
When I meet with family and friends the conversation is about
who has died, or who is that kid next to you and why are they so
big? Then I come to a conclusion, I am getting old
It does not feel that way.
The days seem the same, I still thinking as I used to,
but the reflection in the mirror paints another story
that I am getting old.

VALOR OF THE YOUNG

Let this show that we, young and full of life,
reaped every morsel of happiness out of our lives.
We will gather in old age with smiles of memories
so vivid that the joy will bring back youth to our day.
The splendor of a rising sun,
the rhythmic sound of waves at our doorstep
and the joy of good company.
Even in tropical showers there is beauty
in the abundance of rainbows.
The blood will rush through our veins like rivers,
and the smile that comes to your face,
as only the young would have cherished this,
for it is fleeting.
The valor of youth.

THIS TREE

I know this tree
I sat here as a child
Wondering what is to come?
This tree that shaded my father's father,
who as a child wondered what is to come?
A cool breeze coming off the ocean in a mid-day sun
Here I am now thinking what is to come?
The sun slowly goes west to sleep and left me here under this tree
Wondering what's to come?

HER

Here is the woman, who in my darkest days, and with
loving hands, nurtured me and guided me to adulthood.
For that I am grateful.
Though not kin of blood, she is a mother to me.
In my most formidable years, etched in my soul,
that color does not deny content.
Those lessons learned made me into the man I am today.
The love I hold in my heart for her,
is as if she had borne me into this world.
My love for her, without question, will endure.
White as snow, and with a caring, loving hand steered
me in this blighted world.
Unaware that our resemblance, though so different,
are the same. We are human.
Love should be given as it is felt.
Blessed are your days on this earth and
my heart will mourn you when you shed that skin.
Mother of mine.
There will always be love here for you.

THE SEED

Words are planted when we are young
like seeds on the floor of a forest, where sunlight is dim.
We reach with every word to claim what we crave.
The growth we want to see beyond the canopy we call home.
Majestic in our reach.
What once was like a dream,
we see now how vast the world is.
So much to reach for other than the sun,
now we reach for the stars.

IT'S ONLY FEAR

It's only fear when you lay yourself bare.

That nauseating feeling that creeps up from your stomach

and holds you steadfast.

The words come in layers, but without form,

and you are removed from the reality of what you are facing.

It's all the emotions that you wrangle with daily,

that help you manage a life filled with shards of doubt.

The cuts will heal; but the scar remains.

The strong will nourish their scars and

they will serve as a reminder that you are strong.

The weak will perish and be torn apart.

Fear is just an emotional reaction to a reality gone askew.

It's only fear.

SAME DESTINATION

We are an unlikely pair of friends.

Yet our path seems to have the same destination.

Through the banter and reflection on our lives far away,

through the anguish, we persevered.

Yet we are going to the same place.

How is it that upbringing and wealth, or lack thereof,

we share the same dreams?

Every step in our lives we have fought for the things

we were told we could not do.

Not smart enough.

Not dedicated enough.

Never good enough.

Yet you and I have forged a life with wins that we never expected.

Even if you are not my brother, you are the one that makes me

want to believe there is more to me, and there is more to you.

As the years go by, and we compare notes of loss and gains,

I will find joy in knowing I am not alone in my quest to

discredit the words of my father.

For we have forged a path that is uniquely our own.

There is more to the success we reap.

You, a condor who sees past the horizon,

wise and with depth.

Me, a weaver of words that conjure up emotion.

The past is the past,

and our future is bright with promise.

Author's Note: Sometimes you meet someone who shares so much of what you went through in life its like meeting a sibling. I wrote this for my friend Enrique, and if you met him, you would think we have nothing in common, but our life's journey has been identical. To my brother from another mother. Stay gold. This is for you Enrique.

FRIEND AND LAUGHTER

There is no better pleasure than the laughter of friends.
Communing in a place where the burden of everyday life
comes to a halt, and the grains of truth are picked away.
The meaning of family becomes clear.
To have people who care for you
for no other reason than who you are.
I find that pleasure here,
seated across from friends,
sharing the journey and relishing that moment.
So simple, yet the joy it brings.

DON'T SAVE ME

Give no offerings of hands soaked with blood
trying to save me.
I know what you did.
You changed the landscape on which I walk.
The glory and reverence of peace
is not something that you should utter.
I know what you did.
The other hand that you hide behind
holds the weapon that has slaughtered my people.
Killing them.
"In the name of the father,"
Whose father are you referring to?
I know what you did.
Throughout the centuries you have
laid bare your intent to nullify us.
Make us wither like leaves on a late autumn day;
falling and turning to dirt.
I know what you did.
Collected in ghettos and barren pastures

to seed descent.

I know what you did.

Yet we endure and gather ourselves,

what's left of us,

with grace as humans knowing the truth.

Because, we know what you did.

Manual Labor

A man who works with his hands
caresses the face of God and sustains his creations.
The care we take, and the intricate nature
to sow a harvest from our labor.
A gardener, with seeds that he sows
to grow to maturity and bear fruit to sustain life.
The builder, with every brick and board
brings to fruition a home with walls to call a shelter.
A tailor, whose imagination and skill shows another
beauty that is hidden in its seams.
A man that reaps a harvest with sweat on his brow and body, bears
the pain of his labor and should be rewarded.
His profession is to be lauded for his duty, there is no shame in it.
A whisk of a brush to capture the beauty that surrounds us.
A photographer, who can make time stand still.
Time spent toiling at his craft without him,
we would surely die of starvation of belly and soul.

Author's Note: All my life I have done manual labor and wanted to praise those who build and make things. People who get up early in the morning and help make the world go around. This is for all the underappreciated people. Thank you and I see you.

THIS WORLD

What majesty we behold
when the sky reveals itself
and points a sparked finger
at the land we walk on.
Striking with a flash of light.
A loud reminder that we are
watched from the heavens.
The torrent of showers is like tears
that reach the root of all that is here.
Quenching all our needs.
In that moment we know that
we are of this world and only the heavens care.

PET

There is no greater show of unconditional love than
the love of a pet.
They are there when we are in need of comfort.
Warm to the touch.
The selfless love that they covey in every moment,
The brightness and clarity they bring to our lives,
They are our counsel when the world needs to go away.
The look in their eyes that says without words
the love that they feel for us.
Our pets
Walks in the woods, the park or a Sunday afternoon drive.
Tail a wagging, nose to the wind.
Our companion
Our pets
The soothing feeling of good company on a cold rainy night,
Their furry bodies curled up at our side.
Where would we be as humans without our pet?

DON'T GO TO STRANGERS

Don't go to strangers child,
I am right here.
Even when we don't see eye to eye
I am here.
When life is in turmoil and
the world is at your doorstep.
Don't go to strangers child,
I am here.
My love will keep you warm
and offer you comfort.
It may be all I have to give.
Don't go to strangers child,
I am here.
Even when I am no longer around,
my spirit will guide you,
because I don't want you to go to strangers child,
I will always be here for you.

GONE

Tomorrow when the sun filters through the
open window and the birds chirp a merry tone,
I will reach for you, and the rhythmic patterns of your
breathing that I have grown use to will be filled with silence.
For you will be gone.
Though it is brief and with the knowledge
that you will be back soon.
The normalcy of your smell.
The warmth of your touch.
And the early morning ritual which we both share of
you waking up next to me.
The pleasantries exchanged,
kisses
Coffee made to your liking.
It will be filled with the void that you will not be there.

IN OUR WEAKNESS

What grievous deed we commit when we
bear false witness unto ourselves.
We hide in plain sight and days are painful,
until in our sanctuary in the company of friends
we unveil all we carry.
The burden sometimes slight.
The burden sometimes we battle to uphold.
In those quiet moments, in company of true companions,
we reflect, and tears that are never shown to public eyes,
are released like torrent floodgates.
I know those pains.
Society forces us to shun our true selves
or be scrutinized for our folly.
We are not sheep built from the same cloth.
Our weakness, though flawed at times, are ours to carry.
And that burden is universal.
We are all journeymen in this life.
If we bear our souls and admit your strength is my weakness,
my weakness is your strength,
I will carry you my brother when you are at the edge of failure
I will carry you my brother as you have carried me.

SON

Bear me no malice for what I do and say to you,
I do it with conviction.
Fatherhood has been the only true profession
which I wish to excel at.
Only when I saw you gaze at me,
and with unblinking trust,
allowing me to carry, toss, feed, reprimand,
that I knew I was truly a father.
Years gone by in my role as an uncle, brother, friend.
Not knowing that the endearment that was
exchanged in those transactions were but minuscule
to what I had for my children.
If I think my life has been without meaning,
I pause and remember my legacy.
No matter what it is,
may it be in fortune or words said in earnest.
Be careful how you approach this world my child.
I have been there.
Do not tread too far to the edge or you will see the danger

that I have shielded you from over these years.
My back does not grow weary carrying the burden
of the life I had lived in service to you.
For you will not bear it my child.
As long as I breathe the air that you breathe,
I will protect you and wish no compensation but to know
I will die in high regards.
As a good Father to you.

It's Going To Be Alright

Fresh the smell of morning dew that gathers on my windowpane.

Thank the gods for letting me see its wonders and grace again.

With watchful eyes the sun will rise with precise timing too.

A miracle that never fails to shine on me and you.

My wish today as my day begins.

The voice of my angel beauty sings.

Now I must start my day

I'm on my way

with joy in my heart so full.

The thought of you now lingers there

as I do my morning chore.

And hope that you will think of me as I do from now and

evermore.

Thank You, Please

One day your life will be saved and the joy and sorrow of saying
these words will make you grasp the meaning.
Thank you and please.
When all is given and nothing is expected
the reward will be, thank you.
When the pain is unbearable and life is in dire straits
the payment will be, thank you.
We are not meant to be without others,
and the transaction we cherish most when money is of no capital
will always be, thank you.
When we are hindered by everyday plight,
when the will and energy is not there,
we reach out and ask, please help me.
With empty hands outreached and tears that ask for mercy,
we find the word please, the only value we then possess.
We journey not alone in this life,
and in that journey, like words told to me by my grandmother.

You could go around the world and back with these simple words.

Please help

Please help

Please help

Thank you

Thank you

Thank you

WHICH ROAD TAKEN

When you come to two paths that merge,

take the road less trodden.

There may be obstacles,

valleys and rivers greater than the mind can bear.

But, in that journey, the truth of self will be revealed.

The comfort of life is a mirage,

that when challenged,

separates the weak from the strong.

Take the less traveled road my friend.

We are not born of monotonous behavior

but what we know that brings us comfort in this life,

becomes usual and stable.

FOR BETTER OR WORSE

When we form a union with someone and say the words "I do,"
we pledge everything that ails and satisfies us,
and the joy and happiness which it brings.
Only when it ends do we see the true character of the union.
Most will make excuses and forfeit their vows.
My intention will always be to stay and enjoy every granular
aspect of my partnership.
I see no burden when I make those promises,
because if the spirit and flesh is alive,
it is my duty to sustain it, even when faltered.
That to me shows true commitment.
When a flower loses it petals
do you uproot it and toss it aside?
When a child disappoints you
do you abandon them or recalibrate their needs?
When a spouse or partner diminishes in old age,
and all the outwardly beauty
that you once adored in courtship are gone,
do you move on to what is new and gleaming?

Then what is the purpose of the union other than a
selfish fantasy and means to get the fruit before
it becomes stale and sour.
Relationships are not disposable.
Like a Gardner,
it is to be tended and nurtured.
If it gives you flowers or remains barren,
it is your garden to keep.

LAST RITES

You never know when that time will come
Yet in a fleeting moment the reminder is there.
Crossing a busy intersection
or stepping out your door.
The reminders are vivid,
and you realize, though fleeting,
it could be my time.
All the dreams that have not come to full fruition,
flawed and incomplete haunts me.
Remember that plan you had to travel?
Start a business?
Get that degree?
Call that friend?
Right at that moment it all comes back.
I am not promised another tomorrow,
Another hour,
Another minute.
My last rites were not written because the
whole of me is still incomplete.
These are the times when I am at the mercy of the gods that I
never knew well.
I ask, give me more time lord.
Give me more time.

The Sea

The sea is calling again.

The waves break on the shoreline in the morning and my restless mind will not slumber because the sea is calling again.

Haul up the Main sail! Set out the Jib!
because the sea is calling again.

Check your telltales, snap on to the lines
because the sea is calling again.

Check your forestay, tighten your halyards
because the sea is calling again.

Unshorn your lines from the mooring, pull up that anchor and motor out the harbor to the channel for the sea is calling again.

Tell your neighbor you may be gone for a while.

Leave a note for your wife for the sea is calling again.

Steady your wake in the channel, head on through the breakers, set your course to nowhere because the sea is calling again.

Sun gleaming on the water and going for a close haul
because the sea is calling again.

If I should die now on this body of water, it would be like heaven, for the sea is calling again.

COMPLAINT FILED

We are a nation of complainers.
We complain when coffee poured in paper cup is too hot, yet
complain also when given warm to the touch.
We complain that the weather is too hot,
and as the seasons change we wish to live in warmer climate.
We complain that we should congregate to protest
but only for the things that align with our thinking.
We complain that women have a right to their bodies,
but the choices are left to a governing body.
We complain that places were we live is not the same as before, but
fail to maintain or advocate for improvement.
We complain that churches are good, but don't hold those who
commit crimes against children responsible.
We complain about the technology that rules our lives, and invade
our private spaces, but beg for it when our lives are in danger.
We complain about the kids today
and yet we were those kids not too long ago.
We complain about the poor as we hoard our wealth,
and give to those who continually keep the poor at bay.

We complain about schools and the advancements they have not
made, but balk at the price to get there.
We want so much, and so much is given,
yet we complain it's not enough,
we want more.

REDEMPTION

Where should a man go for redemption?
When the places we hold gospel in are wrecked with
condemnation. The sanctuary the lost go to huddle in prayer,
and be anointed, places that were built to save us.
Men, who frocked with holiness, have clear communication
with the almighty, a conduit to the afterlife.
We cling to a hopefulness that will redeem all worldly sins,
They are not holy anymore.
Racked with the afflictions of normal humans and
asking for the same forgiveness we seek.
They are not holy anymore.
All the coins stacked in baskets passed around
to continue the search for others like myself.
I look around in the nest in which I find myself,
on bended knees looking for hope, or some kindness
and cleansing.
They are not holy anymore.
My teachings as a boy and the fear that it evokes from all the
sermons I have heard in the holiest of spaces.

Humbling myself to someone I aspire to be close to.

They are not holy anymore.

The bread and wine bitter now on my tongue and the

resentment of time served to a thought that now feels wasted.

I cringe to see how ignorant I have been.

I look at the men, hear the message and

untangle all that is being said, to reveal the truth

hidden there.

Be good to one another.

Love thy neighbor.

Blessed is the meek.

Heaven is here within you.

The message is clear now.

They are not holy anymore.

THE PATH YOU CHOOSE

We are not mired to repeat out father's choices,
we forge a path of our own.
The path we choose is not destined by anyone
other than ourselves.
My father, a man whose particular prowess,
chose to plant his seed on every acre.
A flaw that bore me.
Willingly choosing to be a man without need to justify his deed,
never caring of consequences.
My mother, a woman though dear to my heart,
choose to be single and a rare breed for the time.
My life, meshed between these worlds,
confused with my upbringing and thinking
the path was chosen for me,
letting fate dictate my future.
Only when separating myself from these worlds
I now realize the choice was all mine to make.
You are not your afflictions,
but as they accumulate they set a path,

cloudy or clear with blunders that
become the destiny you choose.

Author's Note: Growing up in a broken home I believed that there was a limitation on what or who I could become. I believed this until I found my way. All the people around me, with good intentions or thoughts of who I was, made me believe my only existence was to repeat my parents' folly.

ITS ONLY WORDS

There are words I could say to you that would make a thespian
weep.
But the energy that it would take to parlay to you how I feel would
be mute.
Mute since it would not be any use to you with your blank glaze,
not knowing in the most elegant of fashion,
you have been lowered to the solitude of the gutter.
Without reprisal.
Since there is no one to decipher your lack of intelligence or dignity.
There are words for you my friend,
but I will just whisper them to you
and see your eyes rattle in that box that you carry around
searching for meaning.
Wondering if the intent is with malice or humor.
The confusion will please me as it always does,
as I smile and leave my words to haunt you.

WHAT A YEAR

It's been a year of will and resistance.

Bodies like a checkered board, line the streets, black and white.

Justice requested for deaths that came

unexplained from what is seen and unseen.

The savior becomes your nightmare, lines clearly drawn.

We gather in rooms glued to the screen.

Wishing it was a dream.

Another black body felt unjustified without explanation,

our prayers for normalcy would be unwelcomed.

This is the year we search our souls and wonder,

"How close can we go to the edge of civility?"

Neighbor against neighbor,

flags wave from the back of trucks and we wonder why.

Why is this happening?

All our hidden outrage televised,

and contradictions of the truth is questioned.

The world looks at a democracy, bashed and bruised.

What we know now, who we really are is coming to the surface.

All norms adjusted as we become wary and numb
to the onslaught of rage from all sides.
We want it to end and hug it out, but not this year.
The distance is established, 6 feet apart or more,
and we look at the widening gap.
Of wealth and a future froth with pending conflicts.
The balance we yearn for is at a stalemate.
The year 2020 we watched a fuse lite the powder keg,
blown apart as if in dreams.
The comfort we seek will have to wait, as wounds
heal and covered faces may reveal smiles of a New Year.

Author's Note: There is so much that happened in 2020 and most of it was traumatic that it's hard to try and relive it without bringing up pain. Like so many people, no matter what class or race you are, there was something painful that you experienced in 2020. And then there was COVID.

TIME

There was a time when I held you close and
I protected you from all ills
And I wondered what kind of man
you would become
Your little hand held mine and I protected you
Now a man, not in age but by consequences
There is a chasm now and I hold the line
that slowly slips from my fingers
The bridge that I built all these years crumbles
I miss the smell of the you in youth
When innocence was in abundance
When I meant the world to you
Now the role I cherish as a father, mentor,
friend is in jeopardy and I hold on to the remnants
of what was built
Hoping you will help me preserve
what is sacred to a father
That bond, That hope
That young innocence to reach out and
regain what could be lost.

FOOD LOVE

From a mother's hands we are nourished
with food and words of wisdom.
We, the young and the young at heart,
cherish those that feed us with outreached hands.
Baby no more; but the love is never weaned.
We will always be grateful to those who care.
And give food for thought.
For that we are grateful.

THESE WARS

When will we learn that young men with vigor, sent to wars, in
old age regret their past brevity?
We build memorials to remember conflicts, but when
the moment arrives for compromise, we gather our weapons.
There is nothing in this world that could replace a life.
This earth, those mothers that bore us weep
at what prejudice and fear turn us into.
We will return to her the same as we came.
Your blood will be mingled with my blood,
for we are all brothers.
There will be no peace,
and more memorials will be built because we have not learned,
war is not the answer.

So

Irrational men who emit
out-worldly words that make me spit
Like dragons that fly
Living life as a lie
will meet their fate when knocking at heaven's gate
Not that I care, people like that will go nowhere
With hope and a dream
Like a fish swimming upstream
I will never give up hope
As long as I keep afloat
What was in the past will not last
I am here to stay
Working and sweating each day
As long as I am alive, I will keep hope in my stride
My glory will come
In the morning sun
There is no place for me to go but up
I am going to fill up my cup
Until then here I stay
Making things go my way.

TULSA

Words have been slung on the stoop lately
Hush child or they will hear you
They have said things that you can't believe
It's all about that night they came from the sky
with ground forces
Government funded
All the lies that have been told
Whole towns wiped out and a hundred-year hush began
Now children of that night in Tulsa speak
in audible voices that were silenced on paper
Generations have profited from the loss of black lives yet again
But hush child they may hear you wondering out loud.
Where is mine?
What am I worth?
What is the value of the bodies piled high in mass
graves without
a marker?
What is the value of those driven out and never recovered?

But hush child they may hear you asking questions

Where would we be now as a people?

Where are the perpetrators that killed my people?

What other secrets do you hold from me not written?

You better hush child or they may hear you speaking out loud.

FUCK YOU!

With my greatest heart felt sincerity I would like
to pass on to you my true feelings
Fuck you!
Fuck you! for all the misery and disparities that you
have imparted to us, whom you came in contact with,
for whatever reason thinking there were redeeming
values to salvage from you
Fuck you!
For endless times that you have regurgitated words
which you have tried to show that you have the capacity to feel,
to love, to be remembered
Fuck you!
From me and all the people whose lives you have slighted,
with all the intentions to do what's best for you
Fuck you!
Because we have become woke and aware of your games
and charades that you hide behind.
The fake tears
Meaningless jabber

Starts to reconcile with ones you hurt
All your seeds have turned against you;
we see you now.
Fuck you!
For the endless days we spent in your company and the theft of
money, time and all the wasted moments we had to endure you.
Fuck you!
In the most Zen-like fashion, because there is no meaning to you
but the darkness that surrounds you. An empty soul whose only
purpose is to bring harm to the ones who stare too long at the
mess in front of them, that is you.
Fuck you!
As damning as a biblical verse set in Revelations,
for there is no equivocal blight than you
Go now and never cross my path,
Never utter my name
Never make reference to me or have me be
part of any vocabulary
that comes from your mouth
May this be the last we speak
Now truly
Go Fuck yourself!

*Author's Note: This poem was meant to be sent to someone who wronged
me and I had all intention of sending it. But, I realized it would break
her, plus it was too good to send to her. Well, here it is in all its raw, and
subdued rage. And I still mean every word of it.*

I Checked

Last time I checked I was of a noble people.

Dark in hue, but proud.

Proud of the way we carry ourselves.

Sometimes loud, because we have not been heard.

Sometime with a little bit of self-mockery,

because we have been marginalized and shamed.

We know pain. We know loss.

We know what work is and what we have created.

We love the joy of living and dance to show it.

We celebrate the dead Mardi Gras style.

We remember them.

We carry the load they left behind.

Yet here we are knowing we are regal, but relegated to serve.

We will continue.

For this is a fight, that with each day and

with each win we will regain what we had lost.

Humbled by the journey it took to get there.

Shooting Hammond

My grandfather was a moonshine maker.

My Aunt Dorothy sold shots by the glass from a back window,
because it was illegal to do in the front.

In our kitchen we had a large barrel of molasses
that was thick and dark.

I did not know where it came from, but I knew what it was for.

There would only be one bottle of rum in the house, and it was
never meant for us.

It was for the patrons that came at night, when Christians could
have a shot of Hammond to woe away the pain of hard work and
hard life.

All this was done at sundown so we could maintain the cloak of
respectability in the darkness.

Where judgment was not passed and the water barrel next to the
house was used to wash down the shot of Hammond, burning
with ungodly fire before you headed home to bed.

MY LIFE

All the pain and anguish that we complain about is what builds us
into who we really are.

The expectation is that the value that you hold of yourself is far
greater, or less than, your fellow moronic human.

Yet we know, deep down, that we cannot escape that one constant
that we will eventually die.

Life outside of yours will continue.

All the things that made you special will be gone.

We live life as if we could elude the grim grip of death,
but it's there just waiting.

Watching you squirm and try to elongate what we all know is a
dire attempt to hold on because we will eventually die.

We portion out pain to the ones we meet, and think ourselves
better because we step into the line of wealth and of other good
fortune never thinking "What is it all for?" because
we will eventually die.

The expensive suit you wear,

The house where you try to hide yourself.

All our thoughts and deeds leaving marks on this earth and the soul of the people we meet.

Knowing,

we will die eventually.

All the education and wealth acquired

only gives us sleepless nights.

Holding on tight to such tangible things hoping that it will

rescue you from what we all know.

We all have to die eventually.

How?

How do I say I love you when the world is at your feet,
and all that I know to express that feeling is saying the words?
How do I make the morning brighter,
and the night sky fill with more stars to make you happier?
How do I add to the meadows, filled with flowers,
when there is no more place to show beauty?
How do I find the words to express how it feels when you are gone
for a moment, and it feels forever?
How do I find more ways to realize how fortune has shined on me?
How do I know there is nothing here in this world, or beyond,
that could express how I love you?
How do I go on with my day without thoughts of you
and smiling of the memories you bring?
How am I going to find more joy in this world
than what you bring?
How will my heart heal with the thought of losing you?
How can you love me as much as I love you?
How are my words going to convey all that I feel for you?
How do I say the words I love you and make them fresh and anew?

Miss Marshall

When my mother died, Miss Marshall came to my house and tried
to explain to me the events of my mother's passing.
I was too young to comprehend the loss then,
I only realized that the usual things that had once brought me
comfort were not there anymore.
She was crying, and me blind to the knowledge of loss,
tried to understand what it meant for me.
I showed her my cup that my mother would make cocoa with
warm goat milk in every morning for me.
My mother would exchange the milk from one cup to another so
that the mix of cocoa, sugar and milk would be blended.
I wanted to make sure she was aware that my mother did this and
I would like it to continue.
That night, when mourning family and friends gathered,
I still did not miss her yet because the loss was too fresh to accept.
I felt no sorrow and it would be years after when it
triggered me to think

She is not coming back.

She is not coming back

She....is .... not coming back.

You

You could have died there in Vietnam, but you made it home.
You came home confused, without parades or claims of valor.
You came home to dirty stares and nightmares vivid.
Like the napalm that lit up the field and forest, the smell of
burning flesh sank your soul and you grew numb to the pain.
All that pain you kept hidden for fear you would sacrifice
the few good days that you had.
You came home and hid in your skin, and covered it with
markings, commentating the days when you were in company.
When brothers in arm meet again, the long silence between you
lingers and the losses are drowned with liquid courage to face the
world you came home to.
You could have died there, but now live in the purgatory that you
now endure. And now they have given you a date.
A time to leave from the wreckage the war has left behind.
The seed that was planted there in Vietnam,
pouring from the sky now shows on the X-ray screen,
like scattered children now coming to claim you.

131

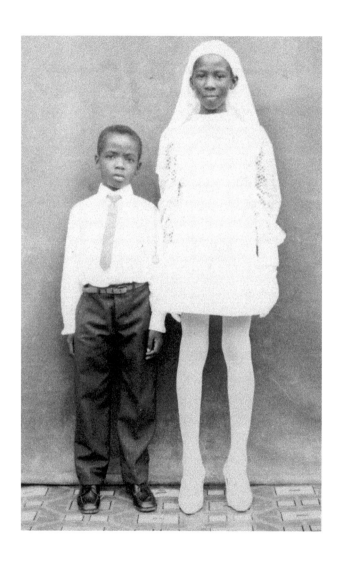

SUNDAY

It's Sunday Morning lord,
don't you hear me a callin?
Here I am howling and a bawlin.
It ain't been easy lord but I am going dress to the nines,
I am gonna go to your house lord,
And beg you for some grace.
It's been a while since you've seen this here face.
But lord I need you now,
Nothing else could go wrong,
I lift my head to you lord in song,
I need you now anyway, anyhow.
Blessed are the meek,
That's why lord I am here at your feet,
Begging you lord,
See me though another week.

TRICKS

There will be no tricks for you to see,
No show of what you taught me to be,
No minstrel act that pacifies your nights,
While you sleep,
and my night terror reigns with the thought of dawn.
I have my ways and I will do what my mind tells me to.
For I was given the same birthright as you.
You are not here to prove anything, if not cohesive endeavors,
To live a life undeterred by another.
Unless we walk the same path,
Hold the same moral justification,
then your existence has no meaning to me.
We were born in the same world,
Maybe separated by geography, race or money,
But there will be a time when our paths will cross
and if you see me as
Different
Less than
With willingness to hold me in contempt just for being here.

To be persecuted unjustly,

I will remind you that this world recycles souls.

This earth,

which we share is a trick.

A trick of the mind that bears one goal

To take us back to it

Back to when we were one.

WHISKEY TONIC WITH LIME

Barkeep give me a whiskey tonic with lime
And I will tell you a story if you have the time
My life was not always like this you know
Let me start from the beginning, back in time we go.
Young man with a fire in his gut
Took to dreaming of America, but with time he got there,
In September 1983 was the year.
Times were tough and he had to push on through,
If he wanted to keep the life he now knew.
He worked day and night to earn a decent wage
And wanted a wife, home and family at a certain age,
The girls were plentiful and had himself some fun,
But decided to settle down and have his day in the sun.
 It went fine as a married man for a couple of years,
But fell apart, although it was one of his biggest fears.
He had a little girl and boy on the way,
Some would call them Irish twins, they would say
It came to pass that he could not hold his seed
Now he had a wife, a girlfriend and babies to feed.

He sucked it up and made the best of it
The good, the bad, he could not quit
He had babies now that he could not lose
Had to go out there, make a buck for food and shoes.
Then along came a Mexican senorita
Bad as hell, I wish I never did meet her
She stole and cheated and took my cash
All the money I had saved, gone in a flash.
When you are beaten, down and out what are you supposed to do?
This was all new to me, I did not have a clue.
Well barkeep if that was all I would have been glad
But she got good and pregnant with a little lad
He was cute as hell and I could not turn my back on him
So, I dug in deeper, and he kept me from going over the rim.
There was a fight brewing and I drew my line in the sand
I went to court to make sure I could keep my little man.
It was a drag out fight, but I won
I could go home and be a father to my son
He grew up fast and it was not an easy chore
He had type 1 diabetes that did not have a cure
I learned a lot and kept him well and good
I taught him things that I knew from my life in the hood.
He is fine now, thanks that you asked
He is a father to Mateo, now a few years have passed.
I have found someone to share my life with
She's a fine lady, a treasure and a gift,
Who takes care of all my needs, great and small
I never again in this lifetime expected to fall.

Things have been good since the year we met
I sincerely love her and have no regrets.
As I go on to the next chapter of my life
It's nice to have a lady like Maria as my wife.
Well barkeep it's been fun sharing my story with you
I just dropped in on my way home for a drink or two.
It been a wonderful life and I could not ask for more
Now I've got to go, as my wife Maria will be expecting me at our
front door.

TRAUMA

We survive the trauma of birth to a world where we are made to conform to a world we never knew.
There is no other word to describe life and the path that we follow.
The screams that we emit as we are forced into this world,
Told to lay still,
Told to move,
Told to walk,
Told to run.
Told to run from one trauma to another.
The pain of love.
The pain of loss.
Physical pain.
Emotional pain
The trauma of living.
Living in need of something.
We try and survive these traumas.
Then, we pass it on and remind the next generation of the trauma we endured.

PAQUITA

In this world we share, hidden in its beauty is you Paquita.

Your compassion and kindness are what we value in this world.

A kind hand that feels the need to give hope.

The life you live is in reverence to the beauty

that the creator intended.

Here you are an angel wingless in our midst.

We are grateful for you and all that you are.

Secular in your thinking and open to all that is around you.

Feeling our pain with outreached hands,

There is no kinder heart.

You have lived a Christian life for the eternity promised.

It will be yours Paquita.

Nestled in the arms of a father that you have given to all your life.

You have given those around you, love boundless and infinite.

Your smile and faith in humanity

will continue to embrace us as the years go by,

 knowing we stood in your presence.

BLACK JOHN

Black John was a cobbler.

A man who could make a spent shoe shine again.

The name Black John was not meant

as a name that showed disrespect.

It described John.

He had the blackness of skin which shined

like polished coal and unblemished.

The reflection on his skin was not warm, but a glow in his

blackness. A small man with a missing pointing finger.

You would think it would hinder him,

but he worked as if that finger was not necessary.

I would go to his home and the space would be filled with the

smell of leather, and in the small shed that was his workshop, he

would be seated and bent over his work.

This simple craft sustained him,

and he always had a toothless smile for me.

An offer of mangoes that grew in his yard.

I saw him last in costume, at masquerade.

Masquerade was something that he did with the same vigor and dedication he had for the spent shoes that he repaired.
Standing there posing for me,
and not realizing that would be our last encounter.

Author's Note: This was written in remembrance of my godfather John, the masquerader. In the Caribbean, most families have a designated person or persons to watch out for the children. Unlike characters in the movies, a godfather in the Caribbean meant they were to make sure that they are there for you, to help and guide you through adulthood. I had 3 godmothers and one godfather. There was hardly a chance for me to screw up. I was being watched from every angle. John was a small man but intense and always kind and caring to me. When I returned to Nevis to visit years later, he would always ask me when I was coming back, and I should save some money and buy some land. Hope this poem did him justice.

BE BRAVE

Gallant is the soul that steps flat footed in the face of adversity,
Never to yield to the oncoming storm.
With each breath, assured that he is on the side of good.
The brave, the strong of will.
He who steps in the way of the just will shed blood
and bleed himself,
But will never waiver from his destiny.

Woman

There is strength and sadness in your eyes
The years have pecked at you
Bit by bit
Defiantly you stand guarded of your feelings
There are reasons
Mouths to feed
Children to take care of
There are no more tears to shed
Life has not been kind
But here you are
The keeper of what you hold on to
The future that was yours,
yet sacrificed for those you bear.

I See You

Harlots in their attempt to martyr themselves
Do nothing but leave behind questions for those left to ponder
What of the god we praise that does not show him or herself and
save the life that was created?
Where are the hands to reach out to when in dire need to meet a
maker that forbade us to take what is given?
A life
A life that with nurtured hands could come to realize the beauty in
this life and the challenges that we face could be conquered if we
reach out
Reach out
I am here to show you the majesty of this world and what you seek
is but a dream
A dream
Of no worries, no pain and castles built in kingdoms of a father
that you have never known
What is known
Is the first light and morning dew
The quiet reverence of nature

The smell of a rose
The touch of a baby's hand
The look of joy in your lovers' eyes
Stay here and see what I see
Knowing that I see you
I see clearly your pain, but it will be better here with me.

MY BEST REGARDS

If you see Jean before I do,
let her know I am sending her my best regards,
she will understand.
For the countless hours spent in her company
and knowledge passed on, my best regards.
The words of gratitude and reflective kindness,
she will always have my best regards.
With a quiet calm and a gentle presence without judgment,
my best regards.
If these words seem simple enough
Let it be known they are said with sincerity.
Please let her know her biggest fan sends
his best regards,
she will understand.

My Prayer

When pity falls like torrent rain,
Clasping hands to ease the pain,
Bow our heads in passive fear,
A prayer for those who are not here.
Those we love we huddle close,
Most eminent pain we deal with most,
The air we breathe in gasp and start,
And treasure those close to our heart.
The joy today that sunshine brings,
And to his name our voices sing,
Careless hope is in our thoughts,
The warm embrace our bodies sought.
The gift of life and pleasure brings,
To him we pray our mighty king,
My lord, my father, I pray to thee,
We are blessed for now until eternity.

I Am Not Sure Of Anything

My friend, I am not sure of anything anymore.
The sun that rises in the east and sets in the west,
May not rise tomorrow.
The love that we nurtured and built with kindness and care,
May not be there tomorrow.
You are not promised the air that fills you with life
and keeps you steady and upright.
Tomorrow may be the day, the body that in years gone by,
had fulfilled its daily functions may leave you.
Stooped and gasping.
There is no promise land or promises that are iron clad that cannot
be taken away.
We wake and, in this life, accept the joys of the moment.
We gather our pains and lay them out,
smiling for what was already given.

My Soul Sings

Memories are like scars, and some heal so you can touch them and they will not hurt.

With music, it made the pain less painful, as I recall the flow of music that shaped my life.

Ray Charles singing, "It's crying time again, you're going to leave me," or listening to Jim Reeves at Christmas. And Hank Williams, "I have the feeling called the blues."

I grew up on all this, a black boy far away from where these songs originated, but my mother loved them, and she played them until they skipped.

The grooves in the vinyl worn bear from being played over and over again.

I remember these songs and now I understand
where my soul came from.

New Discovery

Fuck you! and the ship you came in on.
The Mayflower and those 3 ships, the Pinta,
Nina and Santa Maria. We were here all the time.
Civil in our deeds and culture.
You coming in peace brought violence and death to our people.
To teach us what?
That your god, filled with greed and destruction,
plunder our culture close to Mother Earth?
The God that you claim will protect us never mentioned us in
their books as nothing but savages and slaves.
Columbus should have stayed the fuck in Spain and the world we
live in now would be the paradise you preach of.

BACK THEN

Patent leather Sunday shoes that shine from black polish.

Wool Suit built for cold weather,

worn with a clip-on tie on a summer's day.

Preacher putting the fear of God into our young minds.

The quiet walk to and from church.

Too hot to think.

The Bible verses that came like merciless swords

at night from revelations.

Tearing off those clothes and getting outside

to play marbles with my friends.

Sunday dinner that was started early morning to be eaten after church.

The dark nights on the stoop listening to elders tell ghost stories.

The full bladder that would have to wait until morning

because of that jumbie ghost under my bed.

The shame in early morning, hiding the spot

where I could not hold it anymore.

Gunsmoke TV show seen from a veranda

on a 13-inch black and white TV.

Leaving after Gunsmoke ended and having to

beg Grannie to be let in at night.

Early morning water runs and taking care of the animals.

Pressed uniforms and shoes that don't fit.

Having hands checked before class.

Dusty knees from pitching marbles.

Tucked in shirt, khaki shorts and

dogeared books covered with Kraft paper.

Classes under the tamarind tree at the end of a cricket field.

The open pit bathroom stall that had to be checked for roaches.

Squatting over that pit with the fear of what's below.

The wood trim writing slate because paper was too expensive.

The open classrooms with a headmaster podium.

The hush when someone was getting spanked by the principal.

The rush home to have lunch.

Lunch was roasted sprat fish and dumplings or roasted sweet potatoes. Lime and raw cane sugar with the stalk floating on top, mixed to wash it down.

The rush home to get out of that uniform.

Running bare foot and not caring.

Picking acacia thorns from my feet.

Mango, soursop and guava hunts in the woods on Saturdays.

Catching bees in a matchbox to listen to the humming wings.

The smell of salted fish hanging on a line with flies everywhere.

Dragging your mattress made of "bed grass" in at night.

Sounds of frogs and crickets as your lullaby.

Showering from a bucket of water in an open yard.

Feeding the pigs with "hog meat" Bush.

The many waters run at the source.

One bucket on your head one in your hand.

Playing in tall grass catching fireflies at night.

The star-filled sky at night.

Adults doing shots of Hammond rum and smoking triple 5 cigarettes on the stoop.

Drinking rainwater from a drum filled with mosquito larve.

Reading by streetlights at night.

My love for books, even back then.

Your Conscience

Your conscience may appear clear, yet I bear your name.

Remember the one you gave me?

Smith, Johnson, Allen, Jones.

We live with the brand of ownership ripped from my ancestors.

We carry your name with us.

Our history diluted into what you interpreted and failed to understand.

Years of a ravaged people, indigenous to Africa and the America's.

Holy wars that tell us of a heaven in servitude.

Although cursed in Genesis we accept our destiny and hold on to our faith that is not ours.

It will be better soon they say.

There is a place prepared for you in heaven when you die.

Our pain means nothing in this life and the hope of death is the only comfort.

We are preparing a place for you, they say.

Slaughtering our people with crusaders in the name of a father that disowns me and leaves me to suffer in this life.

Have faith they say, it will get better.

Yet year after year when solutions are put forth,

we are denied a seat at the table.

What of your conscience?

How do you sleep with the knowledge that like dogs, we are

hunted and all that we owned you coveted?

You Judge Me

You judge me from the day I was born.

You make assumptions of criminal intent.

You judge me although I have years of peaceful and painful existence in your presence.

You judge me walking down our streets.

You judge my upbringing, although not filled with a privileged education or inheritance never to be received.

Those 40 aces and a mule.

You judge me for the clothes I wear and the way I look.

You judge me as if I don't belong, although I worked hard to get here from the grip you hold steadfast on my ascension.

You judge me with my mop in my hand cleaning your spaces in your comfortable existence.

You judge me in the fields that you employ me.

Never asking how I got here, but yet you still judge me.

You judge me on the bus that I ride, huddling your purse closer.

You judge me in the stores when I wander in to inquire, just like you.

You judge me in my job, questioning my intelligence.

You judge my worthiness.

You judge me although my forefather's blood is at the root of all the wealth you acquired.

Who judges you?

ANOMALY

You don't belong here can't you see?

Look around you nigger,

This isn't your part of town nigger.

Go back to your country and don't come back here.

In my good-natured way, I smile and nod in cowardice because he is right.

What does a black man do when in dire need of protection, and the protector is not your friend?

We relegate ourselves to our corner and envy all that we see.

That school for your kids.

That small plot of land to call home.

That job when you will be the anomaly.

The uppity nigger. House nigger.

There you are in a room full of others, and you smile.

That disarming smile that says,

I won't harm you

I won't take your purse

I won't rape your women

You: Hey bro, come over here

Me: Wassup my man!!

You: You alright?

Me: I am good and you?

You: Brother man, I need to score some stuff. You got any?

Me: (disarming smile) Man, I don't do that

You: well, you must know someone right

Me: I got to go

You: Is it something I said?

Me: No, I am just not hungry anymore

You: Well, we could play some basketball later ok

Me: Dude I don't play basketball

You: What?

Me: But I do sail

You: Really!!

Me: Yeah, I do

You: I thought you people could not swim

Me: Well, I can, and I heard your people have tails and horns

You: Excuse me!!

Me: Well, I heard it from a friend of mine who told me so

You: I see where you are going bro, that's not cool

Me: So is thinking we can't swim

Me: leaving

The anomaly again.

MY BROTHER, MY BROTHER

You have been told a lie

That lie was told to you in your youth from the day you were free

of that cord that bound you to the mother that bore you

My brother's self-hate is only to deflect from your strength.

That beautiful skin that the sun adores holds such power

That power creates fear

That fear fosters hate

Don't be burdened my brother with that hue

With all that you are, you will survive this life

To be stronger

Self-hate will just bring you to their level

You are strong, black and head held high and proud

This Easter

This Easter in our sheltered space
We bow our heads in holy grace
We give thanks for the life we bear
For friends and family not so near
Things may look oh so bleak
But getting better every week
Giving alms to those gone before
Remembering friends and family at our door
We practice safe distance from a far
But blow kisses, give hugs from where we are
There will be better days to come they say
Happy Easter to all on this day.

GRANNIE

You came to me
Silent at the foot of my bed
With those eyes that remind me of the time I was caught swearing
You never embarrassed me, but that silent look
Unspoken words I knew.
You stood there and without a word telling me to be a good man
Behave yourself
Because I will be here watching.
I miss those times when you would reprimand me with a quote,
"In for a penny, in for a pound"
"The devil's idle hand",
"You never miss the water till the well runs dry."
They stuck Grannie.
And I found myself repeating them to my children
and you are here silently watching.

THESE ARE THE DAYS

These are the days when we, with faceless eyes are confined to our
circle of friends
Where we share fist bumps and hand sanitizers
These are the days
These are the days when men who interpret words written on
paper carry arms into government buildings
Searching for a place to belong and be heard
We hold signs and yell in frustration at what we have become
These are the days
These are the days
Where shuttered storefronts that once employed everyday men
and women lay empty
The uncertainty so strong that it brings a shudder of fear of a
future bleak
These are the days
These are the days when death could be at your doorstep,
and we huddle waiting
Waiting for it to come

These are the days when I miss good company and all the joy that comes in a gathering.

The essence of being human

Hugs are missed

Faces are missed

But we move on because these are not the days to be weary.

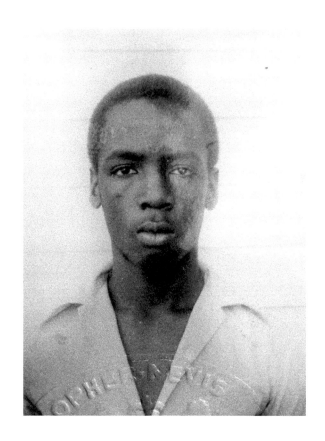

My Blackness

This is not my choice, this skin I am in.

If there is a god, the joke was cruel.

It seeps into your blood, and then every thought is blackness.

There are times when in daydreams,

I wonder if I was forgiven and made to not think of my blackness.

What would it feel like? Where would I go?

Would collard greens and pigs feet disgust me?

Would loss of my daily routine with this nappy hair bring me joy?

Choice of SP 50 or 100 for my fair skin?

Would my loss of slang like "the bomb" or "holler"

seem inappropriate for me to use?

My blackness as it is,

Cursed as it is,

Is who I am.

I am not here for your comfort or words of platitude,

I am here to speak truth and commit myself to resolution.

Undue banter and idle talk,

these words are useless to my cause will be ignored.

I have long been silenced in your shadow.
That coat does not fit me anymore.
I am a voice yearning to be heard since my father's father,
and now me.
Go tell it on the mountain, and shout my disdain for the injustice
and persecution I have endured.
With every word I utter,
I will conjure up the people who have gone before me.
Their bodies ravaged with a life unfulfilled.
I am my brother's keeper and will always be.
No stone will be left unturned,
although hands raw from a struggle too long.
There will be no going back now,
until all is revealed and the truth hurtful as it,
is laid bare.

WE ARE BETTER

We are better than this in our humanity.
We are the hierarchy of life forms,
yet we squander and throw it away.
We are better than this.
In our limited time here on this earth
with nothing to take with us when death comes,
We are better than this.
When color and everyday strife become paramount,
and we lose our conscience way,
We are better than this.
When the land and seas that sustain us
are ravaged by greed and gluttonous need for wealth,
We are better than this.
When buildings go empty for profit,
yet people sleep in parks and under bridges,
We are better than this.
When neighbors plot against neighbors
and we are riled with envious deeds,
We are better than this.

When we ignore the education needed for our children,
or are left mired in debt when pursued,
We are better than this.
When the choices are of life or death when our health is in
jeopardy, and the health insurance company gets
to decide our fate,
We are so much better than this.
Yet we lose attention and move on when one malady is broadcast
for another without solutions.
We are better than this, if we tried.

THE LANDSCAPE

The landscape has shifted
Mother's hold babies tighter
The air is not much lighter
Where we gather in no more
Black Death is knocking at your door
Grandma I miss you
I won't be there to kiss you
Cause the landscape has shifted
Where is tomorrow
I need no more sorrow
There must be a hand to hold
In the card of life, I will fold
I have been beaten
And there is no retreating
Cause the landscape has shifted
Where are my dreams now?
All things have shifted
The Black Death is knocking at my door
As the sun sets

There will be no true bets
That the landscape will not shift below your feet
We are not defeated
We only retreated
Cause Black Death is knocking at my door
The landscape has shifted
but I will not be bested
We have to have hope now
And hide our fear and not bow
Although the landscape has shifted

WHEN THE SADNESS BITES YOUR SOUL

When Sadness bites your soul,

And tomorrow is a dream to remember.

Scars that dig deep to the bones,

And memories will linger.

Tears of sorry will be shed and a wish for sunshine,

Dull with gloom we will cherish.

It's the will to live with future and promise

We will heal, and darkness will pass your door.

Where Does It Go?

In the morning when the first light cracked through the louvre
window, and we nestle one more time.
When the sun sets and the time to come home to you
seems so distant
Where does it go?
When laughter and sadness merge and we are both still there
present for all of it.
Where does it go?
When the simple things that words of joy could not measure.
It should be forever but life, and living, tear us apart.
Where does it go?
When we look back with memories, fondness and otherwise.
It should not have been too long,
but time is stolen from us, and we ask ourselves
Where does the time go?

WHERE WERE YOU?

Where were you?
I thought you would never come.
At time in my desperation,
I had sought the solace of others when hope had faded.
But here you are, within my reach.
Hoping that the feeling is not fleeting.
Understand that I have been here all along.
Weak in my solitude.
I was not the brave hero you wanted.
The damage has been done.
The crusade to you has not been in vain,
Now I can rest within your rapture.

THE OTHER SON

I am the other son.
The son that wants nothing more than the love that she gave.
I am the other son.
The one who remembers where she picked me up and made me
into the man that I am today.
I am the other son.
The one that loves whomever she loves
because she was that mother to me.
I am the other son.
The one whose affection over time meant so much to me and the
memories of time spent together will always be dear to me.
I am the other son.
Although she did not bear me,
I had her love that could not be denied.
I am the other son.
The one whose heart is breaking for the loss of a mother.
I am that son.

Our Love

Like a forest full of trees
Our love
Like a meadow full of flowers
Our love
Like the sound of music
Our love
Like early morning sunshine
Our love
A galaxy full of stars
Our love
A warm bed and you next to me
Our love
The endless memories of you
Our love
Yesterday, today, tomorrow
Our love
Me and you together
Our love

To Be Young Again

To be young again
To behold the simple wonders of this earth
The gleeful laughter of children
When innocence is everywhere
Oh, what joy to be young again

Memories Of Vietnam

Sudden thunder of rain on a metal roof

Sleep coming like a wave over me

The smell of scorched earth quenched

Rhythmic sway of my hammock, back and forth

Dogs curled up next to me

Grunting pigs in the stall,

as they settle in for the night

The buzzing of mosquito's overhead

I want this to stay with me,

to never cease,

Vietnam

SITTING HERE

Sitting here thinking of some witty words
Words that have not been used to show my love
But words do not come easy this time
All I can think of is the only gift I have
A gift of words wrapped in ribbons around a poem for you
Someone so sweet, loving and caring
My humble gift may not be enough
But it is all I have at this time
May this day be the day both of us remember
When the last petal falls
Me standing here unwrapped
My gift to you
My heart, damaged but true

GOING HOME

"It's me"
He looked at me without a word, mouth fell and eyes glazed.
"It's me, do you know who I am?" I asked,
wondering if he would speak with some sign of recognition.
"It's me," I repeated as if he did not hear me the first time. My
mind reeled back to the day I left this house.
Somehow it seemed so big back then, this 2-room shack. Now
here I am again in front of the man who told me to leave,
I was not worth the trouble.
The ceiling seems so low,
and the rooms seem so small standing there in the doorway.
 "Oh my God it's you" he said all of a sudden.
The look of condemnation on his now tearful face,
like that of a man who was about to be taken away
someplace to be punished.
"Yes, it's me Dad, I had to see you again".

Milton Keynes UK
Ingram Content Group UK Ltd.
UKHW040819121024
449514UK00022B/48